*This book is dedicated to my mother.*

Irene Lauretti-von Olnhausen

The information provided in this book is intended to complement, not replace, the advice of your own physician or other healthcare professional whom you should always consult about your individual needs and any symptoms that may require diagnosis or medical attention.

# Wellness above the Clouds

Written and published by Irene Lauretti-von Olnhausen 2007

ISBN-13: 978-3-00-020579-8

Contact: info@itsallinyourfingers.com, www.itsallinyourfingers.com
Photos by Heiner Brackel and Silvia Lauretti-Goldhamer
Layout and Graphic Design by ARTEVI Andreas Rozycki, www.artevi.de
Printed in China

# Wellness above the Clouds

*The unique guide to complete harmony of  Body, Mind & Spirit*

*It´s all in your fingers*

# Table of Contents

# Introduction

*Take advantage of your time on board for a complete Body, Mind & Spirit fitness program that will leave you feeling and looking refreshed, revitalized and beautiful.*

**All you need for this unique wellness program is your fingers.**

The following programs are specifically selected to suit your individual needs.
However, since each of the positions will always help to harmonize Body, Mind and Spirit as a whole, any position you choose will aid overall wellbeing.
In other words, whichever of the simple positions you choose to do, you can't do anything wrong. Most positions may be applied on the right and left side of your body, however there is no need to treat both sides.
„Wellness above the Clouds" is intended as a self-help program, but you may of course use it on other people, for example on your children, if they wish.

**Why do the finger positions improve your wellbeing?**

The ancient healing art Jin Shin Jyutsu® is based on the knowledge that human health and happiness are dependent on the free and unobstructed flow of life energy that circulates through the human body.
By holding specific fingers and/or areas on your body you can balance your life energy that circulates along specific energy pathways in your body. These energy pathways start and end in your fingers and cross at specific points in your body. By holding specific fingers and/or touching specific areas on your body you can restore emotional and physical equilibrium by releasing and harmonizing the flow of vital life energy. The positions given may be applied anytime and as long as you wish and they do not interfere with any other therapy or medication. Each position harmonizes multiple body functions, which is why you will find the same position in several programs.
You should also know that the benefits are cumulative, so that the more frequently you apply the positions, the greater will be your vitality and fitness!

# How do I use "Wellness above the Clouds"?

- Choose the program that best suits your needs. For example: if you are afraid of flying or anything else, or if you experience panic attacks of any kind, the program "No fear of flying", page 12; 13 should be your first choice.

- Most programs give you at least two positions (a.; b.). It is sufficient to do just one, however you may also want to try the other positions of the programs in order to find out which one you prefer.

- Simply follow the instructions given for each position and compare your finger position with the pictures given for better understanding. There is no need to take off your clothes – you simply place your hand and/or fingers above the clothing and keep the position for at least 10 minutes for optimum results. Of course, you may hold the position for as long as you wish! The longer you keep the positions and the more often you do them, the better results you will achieve. If you apply the position on another person, 10 minutes will usually be sufficient.

- Most positions can be used on the right and left side of your body. For maximum effect apply them on both sides, however, applying them on just one side may already show the desired effect.

*While keeping the positions, simply relax. You may even watch a movie, read or have a conversation. However, you will soon notice that:*

## "The way to do is to be" (Laozi)

# Welcome on board and unwind

These two simple but extremely powerful positions will help you to get centred and supply your whole being with vital life energy.
Sit back, relax and enjoy each BREATH.
Unload all your worries while you exhale and receive the purified Breath of Life while you inhale.

a.) Fold your arms across your chest and touch the outer edge of the shoulder blades near the armpits with your fingers. Simply give yourself a big hug.

And/or

b.) Simply touch the centre of the palm of your right hand with the finger tips of your left hand and the centre of the palm of your left hand with the finger tips of your right hand. You may touch both palms simultaneously, or one after the other, whatever feels more comfortable to you.

# No fear of flying

Fears and/or panic attacks are complaints widely known in our times. However, applying the following simple but extremely effective positions will enable you to enjoy yourself and finally rise above your own fears, recognizing them as what they are:

### *"False evidence appearing real"* (Mary Burmeister)

a.) Hold your index finger by wrapping the fingers of your other hand around it. There is no need to grasp it tightly, just lightly hold your index finger and feel your fear disappear.

   And/or

b.) Cross your arms in front of your chest and place the fingers of your left hand in the centre under your right collarbone and the fingers of your right hand in the centre under your left collarbone.

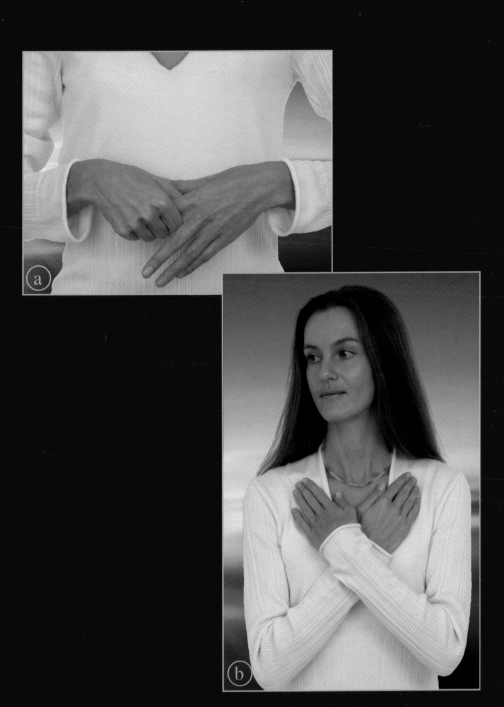

# No more ear problems during landing and take-off

Especially small children may suffer from ear problems during landing and take-off. Simply holding the small finger as described is a simple but most efficient way to solve the problem. If your child or baby suffers from ear problems, the parent should gently hold the child's little finger. To enhance the positive effect of this position even more you should make the baby suck and the child chew on something. You should start holding the little finger at least 10 minutes prior to landing or take-off.

a.) For your child, simply hold both little fingers simultaneously. If this is uncomfortable for you, you may hold just one little finger.

b.) Hold your own little finger by wrapping the fingers of your other hand around it.

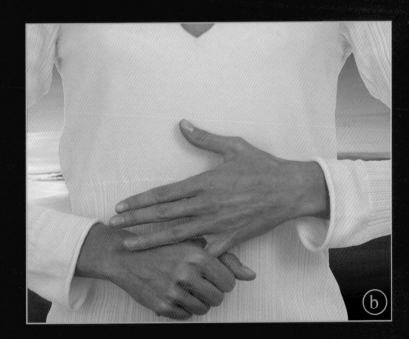

# Harmonizing body, mind and spirit for general wellbeing

Did you know that 14400 body functions can be harmonized and regulated by simply holding one finger?

This is the reason why getting into the habit of holding your fingers as described is a great way to continuously supply your whole being with vital life energy and why it is also very useful in the prevention of jet lag. On a 10–12 hours flight you should hold each finger for 10–15 minutes and you will be surprised at how well and energetic you will feel upon arrival. Ideally you should spend about one hour holding your fingers after take-off and one hour prior to landing.

Hold each finger for 5–10 minutes by wrapping the fingers of the other hand around it. There is no need to grasp your fingers tightly, just hold them lightly, relax and feel your whole body being revitalized.

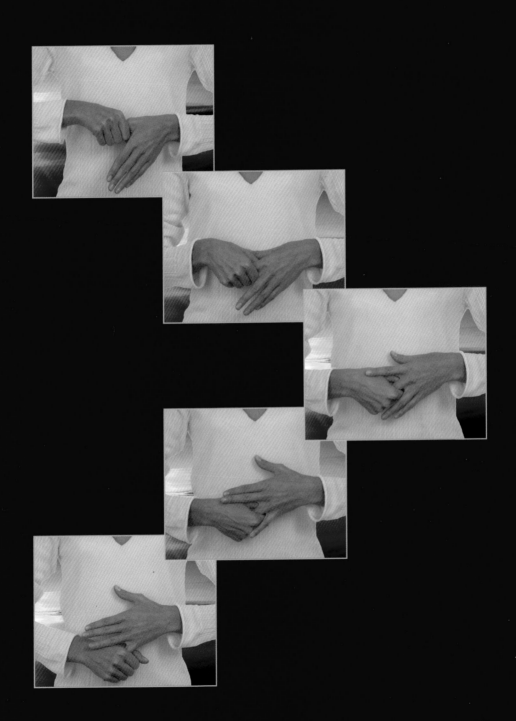

# Substitute for jogging

Experience all the positive effects of jogging without the hard work!
10–15 minutes of applying the following position is equivalent to half an hour of jogging!

Simply sit on your hands by touching your buttocks with your hands and fingers. Keep the position for at least 10–15 minutes.

# Clear your mind

Stop worrying and clear your mind by applying any of the 2 following positions:

a.) Place your right thumb under your right cheekbone and the index finger as well as the middle finger of the same hand on your right forehead, slightly above the eyebrows. Use the left hand for the left side. You may treat both sides simultaneously or one after the other.

b.) Hold your thumb by wrapping the fingers of your other hand around it.

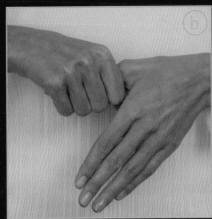

# Instant energy boost

There are times when we all need a quick and effective energy boost. The following position is perfect for that.

Place the tips of the fingers of your right hand on top of your head on the right side of the vertex and the tips of the fingers of your left hand on top of your head on the left side of the vertex.

Relax and feel your body being revitalized and filled with vital life energy within a few minutes!

# Fitness and Beauty

Feeling tired and exhausted? The following two positions will make you look and feel radiant and fit within a short time.

a.) Hold the back of your right thumb, index and middle fingers with your left thumb. Place the other fingers of your left hand on the palm side of your right thumb, index and middle fingers.
Switch hands to treat the other side.

This finger position is an extremely effective harmonizer of the body's vital energy suppliers, liver, kidney and spleen and will make you feel and look younger and radiant within a short time!

And/or

b.) Make a circle with the middle finger and thumb of your left hand (palm side thumb on middle fingernail). Next slip your right thumb between your left thumb and middle finger (right thumb palm touching left middle fingernail).
Switch hands to treat the other side.

25

# Breathe freely

Any breathing problems will be harmonized by applying the following positions.
Positions a.) and b.) will help to free your chest, whereas position c.) is a great help for any nose problems.

a.) Touch the fingernail of your ring finger with the palm side of the thumb of the same hand. Treat the right and left side simultaneously or one after the other.

And/or

b.) Hold your left upper arm with your right hand, and place your left hand on your right inner thigh.
Switch hands to treat the other side.

c.) Hold your thumb by wrapping the fingers of your other hand around it.

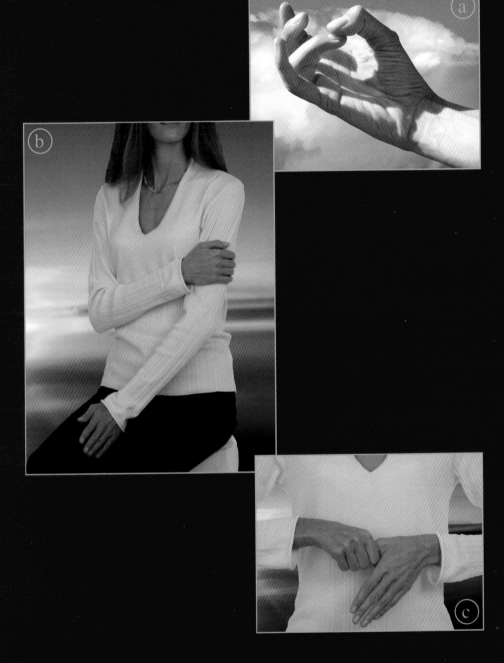

# Revitalize your eyes

Dry air as well as reading and/or working with laptops often cause eye problems such as dryness and/or fatigue.

The following two positions will quickly revitalize your eyes and give you a clear vision again!

If you are prone to eyestrain, getting into the habit of applying these two positions will prevent your eyes from getting tired and stressed.

a.) Place the fingers of your right hand on the left base of your skull and the fingers of your left hand under your right cheekbone.

Switch hands to treat the other side.

And/or

b.) Grab your left armpit with your right hand and place the back of your left hand on your forehead.

Switch hands to treat the other side.

# Calm your nerves and let joy fill your heart

If you are feeling nervous, depressed or sad, these two positions will give you quick relief.

a.) Hold the palm side of the little and ring fingers of your left hand with your right thumb. Place the other fingers of your right hand on the back of the little and ring fingers of your left hand.
Switch hands to treat the other side.

And/or

b.) Hold your little finger by wrapping the fingers of your other hand around it.

# Bloating, swelling, and water retention

Many of us suffer from water retention and bloating when we are not able to move for longer periods of time.
The following two positions will prevent and alleviate these problems.

a.) Cross your hands, and hold the inside of your knees.

    And/or

b.) Hold your little finger by wrapping the fingers of your other hand around it.

33

# Easy digest

Especially on longer trips, digestion can be a problem. To prevent digestive problems and/or to alleviate them, the following two positions will help.

a.) Place the fingers of your right hand on the crease of your left elbow and at the same time place the fingers of your left hand on the crease of your right elbow. Remember to keep your arms relaxed.

And/or

b.) Simply hold your thumb by wrapping the fingers of your other hand around it.

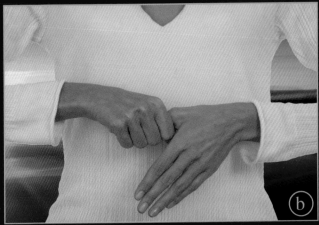

# Fitness for your legs and feet

Even if your legs usually do not cause any problems, sitting for a long time can be strenuous and is often the cause for poor circulation. The following two positions will both prevent leg problems as well as give you quick relief.

a.) Touch the palm sides of the middle fingers of your right and left hands in the folded hands position.

And/or

b.) Simply sit on your hands and touch your buttocks with your hands and fingers.

# Fitness for your back

The following two positions will make your back happy and may also be used to prevent and alleviate back pains when you are unable to move for a long time.

a.) Place your right hand on your right groin, and your left hand on your right shoulder.
Switch hands to treat the other side.

And/or

b.) Hold your index finger by wrapping the fingers of your other hand around it.

# Have a good night and a peaceful rest

Do you want to calm down and enjoy a peaceful rest? Try either or both of the following positions:

a.) Hold your thumb by wrapping the fingers of your other hand around it.

And/or

b.) Hold the base of your left thumb with the fingers of your right hand. Switch hands to treat the other side.

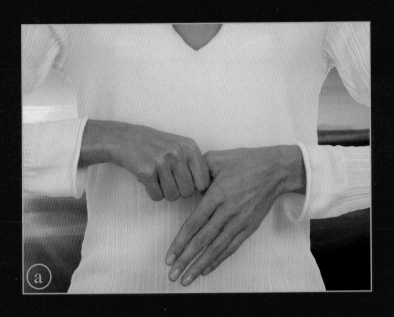

# Stomach pain and cramps

Not being able to move for longer periods of time and eating too much often cause stomach pain and cramps. The following two positions help to prevent and alleviate such problems.

a.) Hold your thumb by wrapping the fingers of your other hand around it.

And/or

b.) Cross your hands, and hold the inside of your knees by placing your right hand on your left inner knee and your left hand on your right inner knee.

# Sudden toothache

Toothaches often occur at the most inconvenient times. The following simple position will help until you can see a dentist:

Hold the index finger on the side opposite the painful tooth by simply wrapping the fingers of your other hand around it.
(For a tooth on the left, hold the index finger of your right hand).

# Soothe your headache

Headaches can turn any trip into a nightmare. To prevent that, the following two positions will give you quick relief. They may be used both to prevent and alleviate headaches.

a.) Hold your middle finger by wrapping the fingers of your other hand around it. Hold the right middle finger first and continue with the left middle finger. Keep the position until you feel better.

 And/or

b.) Hold your thumb by wrapping the fingers of your other hand around it.

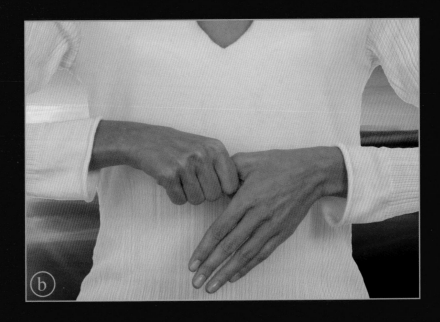

# Happy Heart

If your heart is giving you problems, try any or both of the following two positions. The positions are very efficient both to prevent and to alleviate heart problems.

a.) Hold your little finger by wrapping the fingers of your other hand around it.

And/or

b.) Hold the hollow on the outside of your right wrist on the little finger side with the fingers of your left hand.
Switch hands to treat the other side.

# Nausea and dizziness

Lack of sleep and/or time difference may sometimes cause nausea and dizziness. Applying both or just one of the following two positions will give you quick relief.

a.) Place the fingers of your right hand on the left base of your skull and the fingers of your left hand under your right cheekbone.
Switch hands to treat the other side.

And/or

b.) Touch the base of your cheekbones. You can touch both simultaneously or one after the other.

(a)

(b)

# Anti jet lag and be prepared for a glorious and successful day

These two positions may be applied any time you feel exhausted.
They have an extremely powerful effect of enhancing and restoring fitness and well-being. You may use them either to prevent or to get rid of jet lag.

a.) Hold the back of your right thumb, index and middle fingers with your left thumb. Place the other fingers of your left hand on the palm side of your right thumb, index and middle fingers.
Switch hands to treat the other side.

And/or

b.) Place your left hand on your right shoulder and place your right thumb on the fingernail of your right ring finger, thus forming a circle. At the same time keep your knees together.
To treat the left side of your body simply switch arms while keeping your knees together.

53